Off We Go to the Grocery Store

Avril Webster
Illustrated by David Ryley

Woodbine House 2011

Dedication

This series of books is dedicated to Stephen and Christia,
the children who inspired its creation.

Acknowledgements

- I would like to thank David Ryley, the artist for the series, whose talent, compassion, and sense of humor are evident in all the illustrations.

- I would also like to thank Stephen's speech & language therapist, his teachers, and the mothers of his classmates for their contributions to these books.

First American edition published in 2011 by Woodbine House, Inc., 6510 Bells Mill Rd., Bethesda, MD 20817. 800-843-7323. www.woodbinehouse.com. All rights reserved under International and Pan-American copyright conventions.

Library of Congress Cataloging-in-Publication Data

Webster, Avril.
  Off we go to the grocery store / Avril Webster ; illustrated by David Ryley. -- 1st American ed.
     p. cm. -- (Off we go)
  ISBN 978-1-60613-018-6
  1. Grocery shopping--Juvenile literature. I. Ryley, David. II. Title.
  TX356.W43 2011
  640.73--dc22
                                                                                      2010045382

Printed in the United States of America

10 9 8 7 6 5 4 3 2 1

We are going to the grocery store today.
What will we buy? We make a list.

We park the car in the parking lot.

I get a shopping cart.

I help push the shopping cart.
We go through the big automatic doors.

It is very bright and noisy and busy! It's okay.

I look at the list. Let's find the things we need.

Here is the bread.

I put the things from the list into the shopping cart.

We go to the checkout. We wait for our turn.

I say "Hello!" We put our groceries on the counter.

I help pay for the groceries.
We put the bags into the shopping cart.

"Bye bye, thank you. See you next time."

Hello from the Author

My name is Avril Webster and I am the author of this book. I am married to Robert and we have three children: Stephen, Michael, and Rachel. My eldest son, Stephen, has a moderate to severe intellectual disability (no specific diagnosis). Michael and Rachel are "normal," "typical" children.

> **This book helps your child's:**
> - Confidence
> - Self-esteem
> - Language development
> - Communication skills

I feel passionately about including Stephen in our activities and everyday outings. Like many children with special needs, Stephen finds it difficult to cope with new experiences and changes in routine. I searched for clear, uncluttered books about everyday events, but I could not find any to suit Stephen's needs. With the help of Stephens' teacher, speech and language pathologist (SLP), and other mothers, I wrote this book and several others. Through one of Stephen's classmates, Christia, I met my artist, David Ryley. David is not only a great artist but someone really interested in helping children with special needs. He has drawn the pictures for this book and also created my logo, which features Stephen and Christia.

These books gently walk the reader through everyday events, touching on things that might upset or confuse him (for example, a noisy hairdryer or a brightly lit grocery store). Preparing a child who has difficulty with new activities, changes in routine, transitioning, and anxiety or sensory issues, will help him to feel less anxious and give him the tools to get through upcoming events more easily. Many children— including those with delayed speech and language, an autism spectrum disorder (ASD), Down syndrome, Sensory Processing Disorder, Executive Dysfunction, and ADHD—will benefit from these stories.

At the time of creating these books for Stephen, my daughter Rachel was in preschool and I found they were helpful in explaining unfamiliar events to her as well. My other son, Michael, was learning to read and he enjoyed reading the books independently. Teachers and SLPs have reported to me that the books are also helpful to children for whom English is a second language. They help build vocabulary and language skills, using everyday words to describe everyday events.

Some re-occurring features of the books in this series are:

- Simple text and twelve uncluttered pictures in a predictable sequence. This consistency becomes familiar and comforting to the reader.
- The same multiethnic characters are used in all books so the reader gets to know them.
- Use of a clock symbol to show a period of waiting, an activity that can be particularly difficult for many readers.

These books can be used in a number of ways:

- Read the book at home in preparation for the upcoming event or experience. The words in these books are the words we use in *our* home. Our SLP advised us to use language that Stephen hears regularly. Please feel free to change the text as you read aloud to reflect the language that you use in your home, or omit words that you think might cause your child undue anxiety or confusion.
- Through role play, act out the scenes from the book using everyday items from your home. Make it fun! Trade roles and get siblings or friends involved. You can even videotape yourselves and watch it for more reinforcement.
- Bring the book to the actual event and read it as you go through the experience. Sometimes repeating key phrases, such as "It will be over soon," or just holding the book will provide reassurance throughout the process.

While sharing these books with all of my children, we've enjoyed the intimacy and power of reading together. At the same time, the books have enhanced my children's **communication skills, development, confidence, and self-esteem.** I hope they are as useful to you as they are to our family. Please let me know if you have any comments or thoughts via e-mail at avril@offwego.ie.

Thank you for choosing this book and I hope you enjoy the others in the series too!